T0380867

To order additional copies of this book, contact:
Xlibris
1-888-795-4274
www.Xlibris.com
Orders@Xlibris.com

ISBN: Softcover   978-1-4771-2060-6
      EBook   978-1-4771-2061-3

Print information available on the last page

Rev. date: 10/04/2019

FOREWORD

This book is a group of poems I have compiled on my journey of healing God has brought to my life. When I asked God to forgive me for the life I had lived and to come into my life He did. However, just because I had invited Him into my life and given my heart to Him didn't mean my life was perfect. I had so much emotional baggage from the way I had chosen to deal with life. God made us to have emotions. He made us to feel, hurt, laugh, cry, and be angry. He wants us to use these emotions by sharing them with Him and others in a healthy way. He doesn't give us feelings to shove down into the depths of our soul or numb them with things. Unfortunately, that's easier to do than express them. We turn to alcohol, drugs, materialism, unhealthy relationships, food, and anything else we can. Pain is a part of life and if we neglect it; it festers and remains. We can carry it around for years and it will come out in many different and disastrous ways. God wants us to allow Him into our pain so He can heal us and use us. When I opened my heart completely to Him the process began. I didn't know it would come out in the form of poetry or even that I would write anything down. I do know that I felt compelled to write and I did. I cried a lot. I received relief and restoration from storing years of bad decisions, pain, and consequences. I would like to dedicate this book to my brother William Boling III and my best friend Robin Baird Bramblett. Both of their deaths have made the strongest impacts on my life. William's death took me deeper into sin, muck, and mire by choice. Instead of our family drawing close to God and each other to deal with it we all went our separate ways with our pain. Robin's death and the pain from it caused an awakening in my soul to stop taking life for granted. I had already given my life to God, but I wasn't living like it. I wasn't giving life all I have or the important relationships in my life. I am also thankful for my husband and children who have been Jesus to me through it all. I am thankful that God led me to a church that prayed for me. I am thankful for every person who has been a part of my journey. Those who have hurt me, loved me, or helped me. I am thankful for my pain because without it I wouldn't have needed a Healer or a Savior to help me. In closing, I also want to dedicate this book to the youth. I pray that somehow the words of this book will inspire them not to squander themselves, their time, or their talents for the fleeing pleasures of this world. I pray they will turn to God and do extraordinary things by following His plans for them instead of their own. ** *1 Timothy 4:12 don't let anyone despise you in your youth, but set an example for the believers in speech, in life, .in love, and in purity. **2 Timothy 2:22 so flee youthful passions and pursue righteousness, faith, love, and peace, along with those who call on the Lord from a pure heart. ** Jeremiah 29:11 "for I know the plans I have for you, " says the Lord "They are plans for good and not disaster, to give you a future and a hope. "*

Ecclesiastes 11:1 Cast your bread upon the waters, for you will find it after many days.

A New Creation

Healing Poetry

Steps to Him

2 Corinthians 5:17 Therefore if anyone is in Christ they are a new creation; the old has passed away. Behold the NEW has come.

S
E
A
S
O
N
S

O
F

L
I
F
E

*Ecclesiastes 3:1 There is a time for everything,
and a season for every activity under Heaven.*

Ecclesiastes 3:1
There is a time for everything, and a season for every activity under Heaven.

*S*pecial times

*E*quipped for

*A*ll...to

*S*hare with

*O*thers

*N*ever to return to

*S*o embrace

*O*ften-conflict and love

*F*amily & friends

*L*eft on your path

*I*n life...to mold you to

*F*it into...a divine plan

*E*stablished on earth for all eternity

Carpenter Dad

Psalm 104:23 "man goes out to his work and to his labor until the evening"

Sawdust worn in his hair as his labor was done
Calloused hands I could touch and dark skin from the sun
The days working hard the best that he could
While driving the nails and sawing up wood
Did he know when his day would come to an end?
His family at home would be waiting for him
His one little girl longed to sit on his lap
Then sit on the floor and untie his bootstrap
When she looked up at him all she saw was his face
Did he realize his worth when he was there in that place?
She pondered and wondered if he ever did know
How his children had cherished and loved him so
Did he know all the strength they could see in him?
How they longed to know him and for him to know them
Did he ever know just how special he was?
How the reasons their love was "just one because"
Because there was everything special he had
Just knowing that he was "their" carpenter dad.

Carpenter
Dad

Psalm 104:23
"Man goes out to
his work and to his
labor until the
evening."

Precious Hands (mom)

Proverbs 31:28 "Her children arise and call her blessed"

She would come in the kitchen to gracefully look
The little girl watching her proud momma cook
She watched with delight as her mom prepared meals
She wanted to know all the tricks of her skills
She remembers the banging of the pots and the pans
Her mother started the morning with those precious hands
She would clang and she'd bang waking everyone up
Hungry sleepy-eyed kids who would soon interrupt
The 3 of them eager to eat what they're fed
The little one struggling to get out of bed
They would sit at the table each one in their place
Then mom would make sure that someone said grace
The mom didn't know how the kids took this in
But their hearts were changed in that room by the den
The memories of love and lots of good foods
To cherish and cheer up anyone of their moods
Now as time has long passed and the little girl's grown
You can hear if you listen inside of her home
The clanging and banging of more pots and pans
3 sleepy-eyed children and more skilled precious hands.

Precious Hands

Proverbs 31:28
"Her children arise and
call her blessed."

Distance, *division, destruction*

Intended to break down

Vows and values

Of

Relationships

Communities and churches

Everywhere

Psalm 127:1 Except the Lord builds the house, they labor in vain who build…

Tornado

1974

DIVORCE

"This is what divorce feels like"

Lies of lure

Proverbs 20:1 wine is a mocker, strong drink is a brawler
Whoever is led away by it is not wise.

You were sly when you came to me that summer night
With your poison just waiting to take me a flight
You suggested you'd take me away from it all
You would fill up the void and it's beckoning call
How I longed to belong and your lure sounded great
So I took my first swig I did not hesitate
It took a few moments acquiring your taste
But the feeling you gave came without haste
I had thought about sex and you lured it along
You took inhibitions, every one of them gone
You took all my worries you took all my pain
But when you were gone they came back again
You became an obsession you sure had me blind
No clue of that even had come to my mind
The feeling you gave made me just want more
That living without you became quite a chore
My reputation with you had become one as "wild"
Under all of it though I was still just a child
A child left to herself wandering freely about
On that summer night you had lured me no doubt

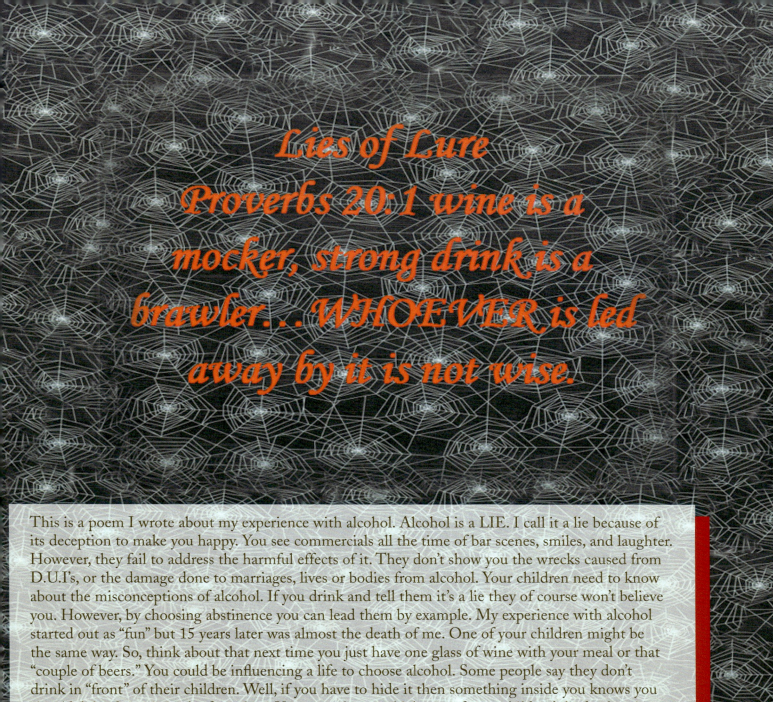

Lies of Lure
Proverbs 20:1 wine is a mocker, strong drink is a brawler...WHOEVER is led away by it is not wise.

This is a poem I wrote about my experience with alcohol. Alcohol is a LIE. I call it a lie because of its deception to make you happy. You see commercials all the time of bar scenes, smiles, and laughter. However, they fail to address the harmful effects of it. They don't show you the wrecks caused from D.U.I's, or the damage done to marriages, lives or bodies from alcohol. Your children need to know about the misconceptions of alcohol. If you drink and tell them it's a lie they of course won't believe you. However, by choosing abstinence you can lead them by example. My experience with alcohol started out as "fun" but 15 years later was almost the death of me. One of your children might be the same way. So, think about that next time you just have one glass of wine with your meal or that "couple of beers." You could be influencing a life to choose alcohol. Some people say they don't drink in "front" of their children. Well, if you have to hide it then something inside you knows you shouldn't be doing it in the first place. You never know which one of your children's body chemistry is going to take a hold of alcohol and run with it. I tried to stop many times on my own and went to rehab several times because of alcohol. It wasn't until I gave my life wholeheartedly to God that I conquered my addiction and the cycles of destruction that came with it. Alcohol=LIE.

Wandering Princess

Isaiah 1:18 *"though your sins are like scarlet they shall be white as snow"*

The night it all happened it was without dare
Just a little girl longing for someone to care
Did this guy know what had already been done?
To the little girl's heart who was just on the run
Running from the pain of a broken ole heart
Did he know all the memories her mind couldn't part?
She was just a lost soul wandering freely about
Wanting someone to love her, just hold her no doubt
No one had told her she was the child of a King
That her body was sacred and meant everything
There was someone above watching over that night
How His heart must have broken over what was in sight
How He longed for His princess to know He was there
He wanted to give her His love and His care
But she didn't know until years had long passed
The night it all happened that it wouldn't last
The feelings would come and the feelings would go
But her Heavenly Father would already know
That the emptiness felt was expected to come
The fleeing moments of pleasure turned out to be numb
How she wish she had known He knew even her name
How He wanted to save her from all of her pain
She lost childhood innocence just like that
Adding shame to the hurt already in tact
Though it's too late for her she can still take a stand
She can tell little girl's of their Father who's grand
He sits enthroned in the Heavens
Loves you more than you know
He thinks you're a princess and
I'll tell you so
He sees your beauty, your heart, and your worth
He even sees pain or well-hidden hurts
So when you just need tender loving and care
Your Father in Heaven is waiting there.

Wandering Princess

Isaiah 1:18 "though her sins are like scarlet they shall be white as snow"

This is another poem that I wrote when God began my healing process. I had hurts I wasn't even aware of. As I wrote this poem, I wept. It took me back to a place where I was so desperate for someone to love me. I was in my youth around the age of 14 or so. My parents had been divorced for some time and I felt like I was going through puberty somewhat alone. I didn't really have anyone to talk to about sex. I was ignorant to what sex really was and was meant to be in my life. I settled for the first guy that came along and made me feel pretty. He was on drugs and alcohol. I was also ignorant to how God saw me. No matter what I was going through He saw me as His princess. I really want to share this poem with all of the youth out there looking for someone to love and be loved by. This is about the night I lost my virginity and bow hurt God was because I was ignorant of His love for me. He saw how confused I was. He saw the pain the divorce brought. He saw the many insecurities I had during those trying years of puberty. He saw my need for Him. Regardless of what was going on around me I needed a Savior. That deep nagging longing that won't go away. No matter how many guys you sleep with, how many beers you drink, how many "relationships" you have. It will be there until you know His love for you and receive it. If you are out there and you are a virgin...hold on!! No matter how pressured you feel God has someone picked out just for you. If on the other hand, like me, you started out with a guy you "thought" loved you, but he left you. Then, you started living in promiscuity and you are feeling emptier and emptier every time you are with someone different. Look up! You are still a child of the King!!! He loves you and He wants to wash you white as snow. His word says that! He doesn't lie! He wants you to know that no matter how unclean you feel that He has a good plan for your life. Call out to Him and ask Him to make Himself real to you. He will! If you are a parent...talk to your children and tell them they are royalty in the eyes of their Creator. Tell them NOT to have sex that God has a special plan for them. Tell them they will be tempted and pressured, but to say "NO!" Don't tell them to use a condom!! That is NOT God's will for their lives! Think back on your life if it's anything like mine. Do you want your child to go through that hurt and pain before they know their worth to God? Do you even know what you are worth to God? Did you have an experience like mine and have some unresolved healing that needs to take place? Open your heart and let God work. He doesn't want to punish you. He wants to make you whole. He wants to lead you to a place of rest.

William

Revelation 21:21 *"the twelve gates were twelve pearls: each individual gate was of one pearl. And the street of the city was pure gold like transparent glass"*

I know you didn't think that the day would draw near
When your sister could answer your poetry, dear
I remember the words you had said about me
The worry you quoted was not meant to be
You see I had struggles and I carried my pain
I even questioned on seeing you brother again
But then a few years ago I found this friend
His name is Jesus and He's my heart's mend
I asked Him to show me a rainbow please
If my brother is in Heaven so I can cease
Cease thinking on where had you been all this time
And so I could have some peace in my mind
Well this friend as faithful as He'd always been
He showed me a rainbow over and over again
So I know without question and I know with my faith
That I will meet you someday at that pearly gate
I will see you walk down that street of gold
You will look in your youth and not in your old
I know you will be there to welcome me in
Because you're there now with my newfound friend.

William

Revelation 21:21 "the twelve gates were twelve pearls: each individual gate was of one pearl. And the street of the city was pure gold like transparent glass.."

BOLING

Talented student dies in wreck

Abortion

Psalm 139:13 *"For you created my inmost being; you knit me together in my mother's womb. "*

Forgive me dear God for I didn't know
How much you do cherish and love babies so
I didn't know that You had quite a plan
For the baby I murdered You made with Your hand
I was living my life for just only me
The world had me blind and I didn't see
It told me abortion was truly *my* right
Even though in my heart there was some kind of fight
I remember I sat there just struggling you know
Do I follow through or turn and just go?
Well, You already know the decision I made
The plan for the baby began to fade
I followed *"my rights"* it's selfish it's true
It haunts me today because I hurt You
I know You forgave me when I confessed it to You
But, I'll need Your help Lord with forgiving me, too
Also dear Lord could You please show Your grace
To the others out there wearing shame on their face
Put people who love You and follow Your ways
In all of their paths in all of their days
Keep them from harm and judgmental eyes
Give them arms to hug and shoulders for cries
Because maybe like me they just didn't know
Your word and Your truth how You love babies so

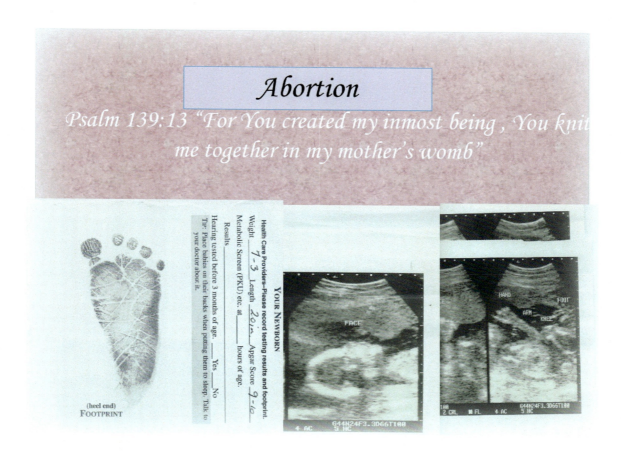

Abortion

Psalm 139:13 "For You created my inmost being , You knit me together in my mother's womb"

I believe God gave me these words of grace for girls and women who have made the choice of abortion and feel disgraced. I know how it feels to be sitting in church or in a group of people and the subject of abortion comes up...you sit there bowed over and your heart is wrenching with pain. Everyone is signaling out this sin and raising it high on the totem sin pole. You are thinking to yourself, "what would these people think...oh goodness if they only knew....would they look at me the same...what would they think???" Well princess, let me tell you what God thinks He is a God of love and mercy and grace. Yes, we have committed a sin, but so has the person sitting beside you that can't stop gossiping about everyone!! God doesn't categorize sin the way humans do. Tell God you are sorry!!! Ask Him for forgiveness and don't do it again. Ask Him to show You and teach you to value life the way He does. If you cannot value yourself and see yourself the way God sees you how can you value another life? If you have had one abortion or you have had more than one...He wants to take You and make You a NEW CREATION in HIM. He wants to make old things pass away for you. He wants to heal Your wounded soul. He wants to take your shame and turn it into shouts of redeeming praise!! You are not alone!!! For ALL have sinned and fall short of the glory of God!!!

True  Love

Genesis 1:27 *So God created mankind in His own image, in the image of God He created them; male and female He created them.*

Recognizing my need for

Eternal change

Depending not on myself or my righteous

Efforts, but solely on Christ and His

Mercy alone to

Pardon my sins and

Take my guilt accepting His

Intercession of death

On my behalf so I can live and

Never die...

My Little Ones (Camrie, Joseph, & Tori)
Psalm 127:3 Children are a gift from the Lord; they are a reward from Him.

Little arms and little hugs
On my shirttail little tugs
Mommy look, mom come here, mom I need you everywhere
Little hearts and little wishes
"Come see mom, come see the fishes"
Little pictures, little hands
Little "play with me" demands
Little kisses lots of love
Coming down, sent from above
No conditions, needs no returns
Little loves continuous churns
Help me Lord just to receive
Little loves you send to me
Stop me in my footsteps tracks
Pour little loves where my heart lacks
Forgive me where I've fallen short
And in my selfishness resort
Forgive me for replacing love
With nags and demands incapable of
Help me to restore your peace
Where there is tension give release
Give me God another chance
To make my little ones' hearts dance

My Little Ones

*Psalm 127:3 Children are a gift
from the Lord; they are a reward
from Him.*

 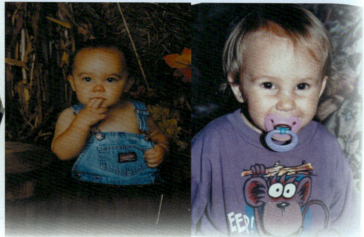

Joseph (my son)

Matthew 18:3 "Assuredly, I say to you, unless you are converted and become as little children, you will by no means enter the kingdom of Heaven.

I know you were an answered prayer you came here just for me
When you were in my tummy I asked God for you to be
I prayed to God most every night wanting just a son
I didn't know that was His plan and it had long been done
And when I prayed I told God I would teach you about Him
I didn't know the chance of that would later become slim
The reason that I say this is cause you are teaching me
I'm sorry the first few years that I didn't really see
God used you very gently to open up my eyes
Cause they had long been darkened by the world and all its lies
He used His touch through you even though I didn't know
That you were just a vessel of the love He tried to show
He had brought you in my life to lighten up my load
He brought you here to show me that and let His plan unfold
For I have learned so much of Him just watching your sweet ways
From hugs and kisses to flowers on those really awful days
I thank- you for longsuffering and for your tender heart
I know it's been a challenge for you to take on that big part
You teach me of forgiveness in a very special way
It takes the heart of God to do that many times a day
You show me what a friend is when I watch you play about
By putting others first-no hesitation or no doubt
What really got me though- is I was listening to a man
He was talking about a cross with a very special plan
He said that God had sent to earth His *one and only Son*
To suffer and to die there cause He loves us everyone
Well as the man was talking *I was thinking about you*
I pictured you up on that cross it's painful but it's true
I tried and tried with all my might to fathom such great love
I realize though like you- it was sent from up above
So as I fought the tears away and opened up my heart
I knew this love had come to me and that it wouldn't part
So thank-you for the part you had in leading me to Him
I see now why *me* teaching **you** had really become slim

Joseph
(my son)

Matthew 18:3 "Assuredly, I say to you, unless you are converted and become as little children, you will by no means enter the kingdom of Heaven

Covered Beauty

Proverbs 31:30 charm is deceitful and beauty is passing,
But a woman who fears the Lord, she shall be praised

Oh dear God how I long to be free
Free from the pain of life's vanity
Why do I get lost in this distant face?
I cover it up and leave not a trace
I put on this mask and think it fulfills
Inside I am dying; this pain it kills
For when in the mirror I do see
This covered face look back at me
I wonder where I have gone
My heart decides to leave its home
I get caught up in trying to be
What the mask will say to me
It tries to define me all day long
It drowns my Spirit; tunes out my song
Make-up here, make-up there
Don't forget to do your hair
Look again what **do** you see
You're looking less and less like me
You cover up what God made real
With worldly desires to appeal
Why can't you just relax and go
Find beauty in your rested soul
God I know this hurts You so
To see me struggle with this foe
It all comes down to just one thing
My make-up is my offering
I want the promise that You said
Where beauty isn't on this head
The fear of You is all I need
I will be praised by You indeed
I'll take some time to spend with You
To make **Your** radiance shine through

Covered Beauty

Proverbs 31:30 charm is deceitful and beauty is passing, but a woman who fears the Lord , she shall be praised.

"Son" Shine On Me

Revelation 22:5 There will be no more night. They will not need the light of a lamp or the light of the sun, for the Lord God will give them light.

Pull back the curtains open the blinds
It's time for those rays to come in and shine
Shake off your troubles shake off your woes
Shine on me "Son" from my head to my toes
Open my mind, my Spirit, my heart
Show me Your hand while I'm doing my part
Thank-you for giving me eyes to see
The "Son" when His rays are shining on me
Fill up my Spirit give me a song
One that will last me all the day long
Keep me from evil help me not to cause pain
Keep my eyes off myself cause it drives me insane
Guide me to where You are needed the most
Then fill me up with Your Holy Ghost
Put those in my path who need to see
How much love is here when You're shining on me
Bless me with love, tender mercy, and grace
Keep me out of the world's continuous race
Just help me to be only all I can be
I'll leave the rest to the "Son" while He's shining on me!

"Son" Shine On Me

Revelation 22:5   There will be no more night.
They will not need the light of a lamp or the light of the sun
For the Lord God will give them LIGHT.

Child Be Still

Psalm 46:10 "Be still and know that I am God."

Why do I always get carried away?
Away from the norm of a simple day
The turmoil of strive is annoying to me
It takes me away from the longing to be
I just want to rest and walk in His way
To experience an extraordinary day
And when I get up to seek His face
Somehow I end up in some kind of race.
I seek and I strive, I strive and I seek
I begin to feel anxious and somewhat weak.
I study, I read, I search and get ill
And all that He says is "My child be still!"
Why do you look for me here and there?
You look in the music, the studies, and the air…
If you will just calm down and rest in me
I can speak to your heart and then you will see
The things I need you to accomplish today
It's only a simple prayer away
I will take you through it step by step
But you'll need Me there you'll need My help
It grieves Me to think you try to do it alone
You use My strength only when yours is gone.
My child slow down give me control
Submit your spirit I'll make you whole.
So when the night comes to an end
Wake up my child I'll be your friend
Come sit with me in that quiet place
And please get out of this "spiritual race!"

32

Child Be Still

Psalm 46:10 "Be still and know that I am God."

33

PRAY

Philippians 4:6–7 "Be anxious for nothing, but in everything by prayer and supplication, with thanksgiving, let your request be made known to God; and the PEACE of God which surpasses all understanding, will guard your hearts and minds through Christ Jesus. "

After a night of peaceful rest
I try to get up and I'm doing my best
The nudge of Your Spirit says it's time for a chat
My body says, "No, there's much time for that"
You say, "It's quiet come and sit with me"
"Start your day with stillness and glee"
But, as I lay there, and ignore You again
Time goes by fast the day soon begins
The children are up there's so much to do
Breakfast, teeth brushed, don't forget shoes!
As I hurry along in frantic dismay
It never occurs I forgot to pray
Kids in the car all ready to go
Look at the time!! Calm down drive slow
The car slows down, but my minds all array
If only I had of remembered to pray
Kids are at school and there's much more to do
I'm thinking of everything, but not about You
Where do I start now and where do I end?
Maybe I'll just phone a friend
Talk, talk, talk and do some chores
In and out of rooms shutting doors
Going to town now to pay a bill
Someone's rude now I'm ill
Go to the store for "worldly" glances
On my car a praying mantis
"Wow!" I say that is SO cool
It never occurred that it was You
Stop and pray my child you'll see
The stress you have will turn to glee
So, listen to me when I call
I want what's best for you that's all
Next time when you start your day
Turn to me and PRAY, PRAY, PRAY!!!

This is once again a true story in my life of poems. This was one of the many days that I started my day without prayer or focus. It was a day of stress in the life of motherhood. When I saw the praying mantis sitting so solemn on my car I was amazed for a split second. Even in the midst of my many distractions I was able to steal a quick glance of God at work in my life. I still fall short of neglecting to pray everyday, but I know the difference now. I have much more patience, peace, and understanding when I am in sync with God. I am thankful for those times. I am also thankful for the times I fall short because they are opportunities to learn.

Facing my faults and

Receiving His grace

Expecting to see

Extraordinary results while

Determined to persevere in spite of

Opposition

Magnifying Him

Instead of myself

Never giving up... on the

Cause of

Him as I

Remember His love

In spite of myself and

Share it with others

To accomplish His purpose

FREEDOM in CHRIST ✝

John 8:36 if the Son sets you free you will be free indeed.

Transparency   Conqueror

Grace   *Joy*

Love   Action

HOPE   *Truth*

Peace   Strength

Perseverance   Faith

Courage

RANDOM QUOTES OF POETRY and PICTURES TO FOLLOW:

The fading of life is sad
And deeper than I understand
The beauty of love when it's gone
Is like quicksand
Help me Lord to love & cherish
According to Your plan
To aid & to heal in the path
Of all my fellow man~

Why so much pain the dark world brings
To the heart of a child
It's better to stay there
Where I once was loved by so many
To find such emptiness…hurts

*REGRET~~a dark,thick,hovering,cloud
covering up what could be now…LOVE

*LOVE~~touched by others so subtle yet
"divine" one day you see it clearly in lost
time.

William~special in your plight… words so few spoken
Yet written to my delight. Why was your stay so brief?
How I long for you my friend, my brother. In my heart
Is your LOVE……05/21/1964-07/27/1985

Robin~stubborn, yet supportive
Loyal until the end…why did I not
Know sooner you were my TRUE
Best friend??? 04/21/1969-09/15/2009

Psalm 37:4 "Delight yourself in the Lord and He will give you the desires of your heart."

38

ROBIN

Luke 17:6 *He replied, if you have faith as small as a mustard seed.......*

Frustration

by Sharon Schwartz on Tuesday, November 24, 2009

Philippians 4:8 Finally, my brothers and sisters, always think what is true. Think about what is noble
right, and pure. Think about what is lovely and worthy of respect. If anything is excellent or worthy
of praise think about these things.

Frustration comes frustration goes
Oh the grip it tries to hold
It messes up and twists your thoughts
Causes anger where peace once wrought
Sometimes it comes but once a day
Other times it plans to stay
If you wish to find a cure
Force your thoughts to thinking pure!!!!!

Short and sweet. For the past year, I have been in some circumstances that I would rather not be in
It has took my focus off of Jesus and what is important (my family/love) more times than I can
count. I am learning to count my blessings....name them one by one. It really helps when I put on
my attitude of gratitude. In life, I have found ...it's not about me, it's not about my comfort, it's not
about what "I" want. It's about what God wants for me. He knows what's best. We can complain
question.. .I don't think He really cares if we do-it doesn't change who HE is or what He is trying
accomplish in our lives. He does deserve our praise for at least one thing (really more) EVERY day
So, if you are like me and sometimes you allow circumstances, people, or your own feelings to
dictate your faith. STOP... look for one thing you are thankful for and just start telling God. You'll be
surprised when other things start flowing out of your mouth.

"Their" Life of Sin...

By Sharon Schwartz on Tuesday, November 17, 2009

Matthew 7:1-2 "Do not judge others. Then you will not be judged. You will be judged in the same way you judge others. You will be measured in the same way you measure others.

Help me Lord to truly see
Your righteousness is not of me
These filthy rags I wear around
Beneath it all is where you're found
Remind me with your Spirit free
That nothing good can come from me
As I look around at others
To my sisters and my brothers
May I not see specks in eyes
But souls You long to unify
For when I see "their" life of sin
My heart lifts up as if to win
Before I know it I'm there, too
For judging them not letting You.

Fear

by Sharon Schwartz on Friday, November 13, 2009

Matthew 14:30 But when he saw that the waves were boisterous, he was afraid; and beginning to sink he cried out, saying, "Lord save me!"

Lord make this fear just go away why can't it just subside?
I know I have to conquer it to reach the other side
For when I fix my eyes on You; my Spirit it will soar
Then suddenly it happens and it isn't anymore
I'm getting tired of stepping out onto the water's wave
Then paralyzed by fear I begin to be it's slave
Forgive me Lord for unbelief that keeps me standing still
Oh father how I long to come You know just how I feel
So as I fix my eyes on You and give to You my hand
Please take me Lord another step into the Promised Land.

The opposite of fear=FAITH
Hebrews 11:1 Now faith is being SURE of what we HOPE for and CERTAIN of what we do not YET see.

What happened?????

By Sharon Schwartz on Tuesday, November 10,2009

What happened to your childlike heart what caused it to decay?
For when I share my heart with you it's to my great dismay
To find that you have layered up your soul with hurts and pains
Distractions from this fast paced world and it's material gains
It really does concern my soul that you were led astray
I long to see the part of you that's mired with muck and clay
It makes it hard to share with you the light that's in my soul
To take you from this covered up and superficial roll
What happened to the way it was when we could all relate
Basking in the hope of love without a great debate
What happened to the times we'd laugh especially times we'd cry?
When we could say, "I'm sorry" and then tell the reason why
I pray the Lord will help us to break down these mighty walls
For it's not just me who's longing it's Him who really calls
He calls us to REALITY to share our hearts and lives
To help each other mend our ways so we can all survive
Surviving life and sharing is what we are called to do
Loving much and caring in a way that's really true
So, if there's love left in your soul I care to truly ask
Just open up and let me see, take off that long worn mask
I promise I'll still be here when you shed your weary soul
For God will use us both the same and make each of us whole
So when the time has come when you really want to share
I will see your childlike heart and I'll know what's happening there.

43

Be still and know I am God.

Psalm 23:2 He lets me lie down in fields of green grass.
He leads me beside quiet waters.

I Corinthians 3:7 "So then neither the one who plants nor the one
who waters is anything, but God who causes the growth"

Sharon Schwartz
2012

In the beginning.....God

Psalm 34:1 I will thank the Lord at all times. My lips will always praise Him.

Sharon Schwartz

Camrie

Me

She's my college
girl<3

Schwartz family

Revelation 12:11 *they overcome him by the blood of the Lamb and the word of their testimony.....*

Printed in the United States
By Bookmasters